DK

LANGUAGE ARTS MADE EASY

2nd Grade Workbook

10 Minutes A Day

Spelling games

Author Linda Ruggieri
Consultant Claire White

10-minute challenge

Try to complete the exercises for each topic in 10 minutes or less. Note the time it takes you in the "Time taken" column below.

DK Penguin Random House

DK London
Editors Elizabeth Blakemore, Jolyon Goddard
US Editor Shannon Beatty
Proofreader Christina Heilman
Managing Editor Christine Stroyan
Managing Art Editor Anna Hall
Consultant Claire White
Senior Production Editor Andy Hilliard
Senior Production Controller Jude Crozier
Jacket Design Development Manager Sophia MTT
Publisher Andrew Macintyre
Associate Publishing Director Liz Wheeler
Art Director Karen Self
Publishing Director Jonathan Metcalf

DK Delhi
Project Editor Neha Ruth Samuel
Senior Art Editor Stuti Tiwari Bhatia
Editorial team Rohini Deb, Mark Silas
Art Editor Rashika Kachroo
Managing Editors Soma B. Chowdhury, Kingshuk Ghoshal
Managing Art Editors Ahlawat Gunjan, Govind Mittal
Design Consultant Shefali Upadhyay
Senior DTP Designer Tarun Sharma
DTP Designers Anita Yadav, Rakesh Kumar, Harish Aggarwal
Senior Jacket Designer Suhita Dharamjit
Jackets Editorial Coordinator Priyanka Sharma

This American Edition, 2020
First American Edition, 2014
Published in the United States by DK Publishing
1450 Broadway, Suite 801, New York, NY 10018

20 21 22 23 24 10 9 8 7 6 5 4 3 2 1
001–322751–May/2020

A catalog record for this book is available from the Library of Congress.
ISBN 978-0-7440-3154-6

Printed and bound in Canada

Contents

Time Taken

Time Filler:
In these boxes are some extra challenges to extend your skills. You can do them if you have some time left after finishing the questions. Or, these can be stand-alone activities that you can do in 10 minutes.

Long Vowel Sounds

The vowels **a**, **e**, **i**, **o**, and **u** can make long sounds in words. Knowing these sounds in words will help your spelling and reading skills.

1. Add the missing vowel (**a**, **e**, **i**, **o**, or **u**) to complete each word.

j_ice

m_at

c_ke

b_by

potat_

kn_fe

2. Draw lines to match the pairs of words that have the same vowel sound.

soap flute size cape leap

light rope peek cube bait

3. Circle the two words with long vowel sounds in each sentence.

Dan made an error in the game.

Ann gave Jon five pens.

The paint was blue.

Time Filler:
Create simple titles for imaginary books. Include as many long vowel words in the titles as possible. For example: *The Huge Blue Whale.*

4 Look at each picture and read the words with long vowel sounds below. Then circle the word that names the picture.

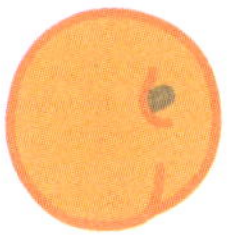		
pine	hide	mile
pipe	hive	mice
peach	high	pile

5 Color the pieces of the pie that have long vowel words.

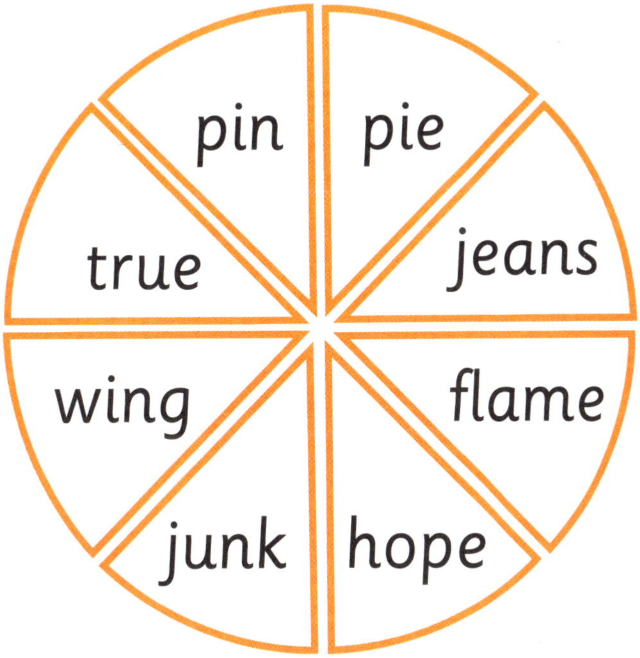

Short Vowel Sounds

The vowels **a**, **e**, **i**, **o**, and **u** can make short sounds in words. Knowing these sounds in words will help your spelling and reading skills.

1 Read the two words in each row aloud. Listen to the sound of the letters in bold. Choose a word from the box with the same vowel sound.

lunch	jog	mad	net	dig

kn**o**b, h**o**t ....

l**u**ck, d**u**st ....

m**a**gic, l**a**dder ....

d**i**nner, d**i**p ....

p**e**t, t**e**n ....

2 Choose a short vowel word from the box to answer each clue.

dog	sun	neck	duck	bell	ball	red

an animal that barks ....

the name of a color ....

it holds your head up ....

something that rings ....

it shines brightly in the sky ....

an animal that quacks ....

a round toy that is thrown, kicked, or hit ....

Time Filler:
How many words with short vowel sounds can you make using the letters in the word "grandfather"? Make a list of these words.

3) Read the six short vowel words in the box. Now look in the word search for those words. Draw a circle around each one.

mess   frog   fox   mix   rush   swam

s	w	a	m	q	n
f	r	o	g	a	l
o	l	m	i	x	e
x	r	e	n	b	p
r	u	s	h	c	h
t	k	s	d	e	t

4) Sort the words from the box under the correct heading.

dream   patch   train   cone   wish   jet

Long vowel words	Short vowel words
....	....
....	....
....	....

The Letter y

The letter **y** can make the long "i" or the long "e" vowel sound when used at the end of words.

1) Read each clue. Then choose the word it describes from the box.

sly	dry	cry	sky

It is above us and is often blue. ....

If you are sad, you might do this. ....

It is the opposite of wet. ....

Another word for "sneaky." ....

2) Choose a word from the box to match each picture.

penny	thirty	sunny	bunny

....

....

....

....

3) Choose the correct word to complete each sentence below.

My aunt wanted to .... a new car. buy/my

She was so .... to find a nice red dress. why/happy

John said he would .... to deliver it soon. cry/try

Time Filler:
The letter y can be tricky! Remember to say "my baby" to help you remember the vowel sounds that y makes at the end of words.

4 For each picture, circle the word that describes it.

silly	cry	dry
try	fry	fly
sleepy	my	sty

5 Read each sentence below. Does the letter **y** make an "i" sound or "e" sound in the underlined word? Write **i** or **e** on the line.

We drove to the <u>city</u> to go to the museum. ....

Father stopped to <u>buy</u> food for the trip. ....

We left <u>early</u> on Tuesday morning. ....

Wow, that fun day just flew <u>by</u>! ....

We arrived <u>quickly</u>. ....

The <u>sly</u> fox sneaked away from the barn. ....

The Long **a** Letter Teams

The letter teams **ay** and **a-e** make the long "a" sound.

1 Pick a word from the word box that rhymes with the underlined word in each sentence.

late	face	shave	fade	tape	shake

I will race you to the swings. ....

Mary likes to read under the shade of the oak tree. ....

I had to wake up early to get to the game on time. ....

Ken's dog jumped over the gate. ....

Amy's favorite shape is a square. ....

They hope to pave the path as soon as possible. ....

2 Complete the words with the long "a" letter teams **ay** or **a-e**.

I will p__ for ten b_l_s of h__.

He wore the knee br_c_ all d__ long.

We tried to tr_c_ the w__ to Jan's pl_c_.

Time Filler:
Choose ten words from these pages and write them in alphabetical order. Here is the alphabet to help you:
a b c d e f g h i j k l m n o p
q r s t u v w x y z

3 Read the clues and unscramble the letters to make words with the long "a" sound.

Clue	Scrambled word	Unscrambled word
a fruit	perag	
we turn this in a book	gape	
courageous	bvrae	
a garden tool	krae	
the opposite of wild	atem	

4 Draw a line from each **ay** word to its meaning.

May — you can make things with it

day — to give money

hay — a month

clay — dry grass

pay — seven of these make one week

The Long **e** Vowel Teams

The vowel teams **ee** and **ea** make the long "e" sound.

1. Help Queen Colleen reach her peaches! Add **ee** or **ea** to each stone to make a word. If you cannot make a real word, cross out the stone. Color the stones with real words to show the queen's path.

2. Use the letters of the alphabet to make rhyming **ee** and **ea** words.

a b c d e f g h i j k l m n o p q r s t u v w x y z

teach	bee ....
team	clean ....
cheek	sheep ....

Time Filler:
Choose five words from these pages and think of words that rhyme with them. Write the rhyming words in pairs. Then use some of the rhyming words to make a short poem.

3) Find and circle **ee** and **ea** words in each sentence below.

Last week, I saw a hive of bees by the stream.

“The heat has made me feel weak,” said Jean.

The screen seems to be torn in at least three places.

4) Complete each picture's name with either the **ee** or **ea** vowel team.

sh__p

m__t

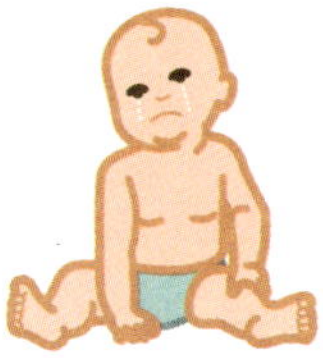
w__p

s__t

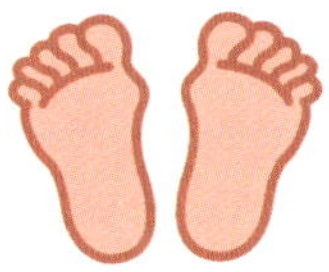
f__t

l__p

The Long i Letter Teams

The letter teams **igh** and **ie** make the long "i" sound.

1 Pick a word from the box to complete each sentence.

right	knife	bright	fries	dried

It was a windy day, so the clothes on the line quickly ....

The sun was .... and warm when we played outside.

The sharp .... sliced the bread easily.

I had the best .... I have ever tasted yesterday.

Sean checked to see if he had the .... answer.

2 The vowel team **ie** doesn't always make the long "i" sound. Sometimes it makes the long "e" sound. Read the first word in each row. Then circle the word in the row that has the same long "i" sound.

fried	chief	lie
life	tries	field
high	niece	ties
night	sigh	brief

Time Filler:
Write a short story about a bike. Use as many long "i" words as you can think of. You can use words such as "light," "ride," "sight," "tried," and "flies."

3 Read the words in the grid below. Color the boxes that include words with the long "i" sound.

pie	yield	tight	belief
shield	sight	grief	high
cookie	die	cries	chief

4 Read the two words under each picture. Then circle the word that names the picture.

flies fight

fried tie

tight light

5 Unscramble the letters to make words with the **igh** or **ie** letter teams.

sskei ....

timhg ....

lfgiht ....

ipe ....

gihh ....

ite ....

The Long o Letter Teams

The letter teams **ow** and **o-e** make the long "o" sound.

1. Write **ow** to complete each word. Then read the words aloud.

cr__ sn__ gr__ wind__

m__ bl__ l__ fl__

2. Fill in the missing letters. Then read the **o-e** words aloud.

gl_b_

ph_n_

st_n_

r_b_

3. Read each clue. Then choose the word that matches it from the box.

row	joke	mow	slow	poke

something funny you tell another person ....

you do this in some boats ....

the opposite of fast ....

to prod with a finger or stick ....

to cut grass ....

Time Filler:
Make a list of some ow and o-e words. Use the list to write some fun rhymes of your own.

4 Finish each rhyme with an **ow** or **o-e** word.

The wind will ....
And the grass will ....
My dad will soon
Begin to .... !

My dog found a .... ,
While I talked on the ....
He took it away
And left me ....

5 Write each word from the word box under the correct heading.

throw	home	elbow	stove
nose	stone	rode	Rome

Action words
....
....

Body parts
....
....

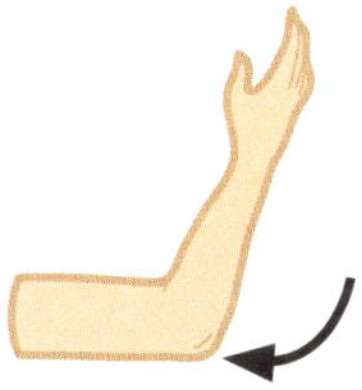

Place words
....
....

Words for things
....
....

The Long **u** Vowel Teams

The vowel teams **ue** and **u-e** make the long "u" sound.

1 Read these words. Then follow each instruction below.

mule rules June

blue cute

Underline the word you might use to describe a kitten.

Draw a circle around the word that names a month.

Draw a box around the word that names an animal.

Draw a dotted line under things we follow at school.

Cross out the word that names the color of the morning sky.

2 The word box below has words with the vowel teams **ue** and **u-e**. Find these words in the word search.

use flute rules clues mule

c	l	u	e	s
c	k	m	p	b
f	l	u	t	e
r	u	l	e	s
u	s	e	o	p

Time Filler:
Make a list of all the u-e words you can think of. Write a short story using as many of them as you can.

3 Choose the correct word from the box and write it next to its meaning.

cube	rude	glue	huge

It means "really big." ....

It is very sticky. ....

It is a shape with square sides. ....

It describes someone with bad manners. ....

4 Complete each word with **u-e** to name the picture.

c_b_

t_b_

fl_t_

5 Write a **u-e** word in each box for each clue.

u-e

melody ....

a hill of sand ....

Useful Word List 1

Read each column of words. Then cover the words up one by one and write them. Then move on to the next column.

able	growl ....
cucumber	climb ....
known	against ....
smooth	rustle ....
thumb	edge ....
bare	follow ....
elevate	agree ....
bloom	pour ....
library	field ....
chief	believe ....

Time Filler:
Make sentences using the words here. Keep coming back to this list to check that you still know the spellings of these useful words.

chirp	....	radio	....
hiss	....	decide	....
idea	....	artist	....
toast	....	special	....
editor	....	though	....
bought	....	balloon	....
neither	....	island	....
o'clock	....	unknown	....
poem	....	young	....
enough	....	writer	....

The **oo** Vowel Team

The vowels **oo** can make a long sound, as in "soon," and a short sound, as in "foot."

1 Say each word in the box aloud. Then write it under the correct heading based on the sound it makes.

loose tooth look proof book hood

"oo" as in "soon"	"oo" as in "foot"
....	....
....	....
....	....

2 Read each sentence. If the underlined word has the "oo" sound of "soon," write an **s** on the line. If it has the "oo" sound of "foot," write an **f** on the line.

The flowers began to bloom in the garden. ....

Please give me a scoop of chocolate ice cream. ....

Jenny is the best cook in her family. ....

His father shook the rug to get rid of the dust. ....

Tina chopped some wood for her grandmother. ....

Faye was so sick she could not leave her room. ....

Time Filler:
Use a dictionary to find the meaning of these words: "loom," "brood," "spoof," "loon," and "croon." Keep a notebook with definitions of these words.

3 Some words are in the wrong place! Cross out the words that do not have the "oo" sound of "foot" on the foot. Cross out the words that do not have "oo" sound of "moon" on the moon.

4 Write three words for each **oo** spelling pattern: **oon**, **ool**, and **ook**. Hint: they're the sounds you hear in "soon," "cool," and "look."

soon	cool	look
....	....	....
....	....	....
....	....	....

Other Vowel Sounds

The letter teams **aw** and **au** make the sound you hear in "saw" and "cause." The letter team **al** makes the sound you hear in "also."

1 Sort the words from the box into the letter teams for **aw**, **al**, and **au** words.

shawl taught fawn sauce halt
caught salt yawn false

aw	**al**	**au**
....	....	....
....	....	....
....	....	....

2 Use the words from the box to complete each sentence. Note the vowel sounds.

bawl seesaw dawn launch crawled paused

To send up a rocket is to .... it.

The children enjoyed playing on the ....

The baby started to .... noisily at bedtime.

At ...., we went out for a long hike.

She .... before she finished speaking.

The spider .... across its web.

Time Filler:
By changing the beginning letter or letters of many aw, au, or al words you can make rhyming words, such as "halt" and "salt." Create some pairs of rhyming words and use them in a short poem.

3) Complete the words in each sentence below. Then find the words in the word search and circle them.

My dog is sm__ler than your cat!

She c__ght the b__l quickly.

Jon helped his father h__l wood.

The cat has sharp cl__s.

c	a	u	g	h	t	e	h
l	p	l	w	s	y	b	a
a	h	b	a	l	l	n	u
w	r	w	n	b	p	t	l
s	s	m	a	l	l	e	r

4) Use the alphabet to find a rhyming word for each word below.
a b c d e f g h i j k l m n o p q r s t u v w x y z

law .... ball ....

fawn .... raw ....

More Vowel Sounds

The letter teams **oi** and **oy** make the sound you hear in "spoil" and "boy." Remember the letter team **ow**? It not only makes the long "o" sound, but it can also make a different sound, as in "down" and "cow."

1 Write either **oi** or **oy** to complete each word.

j _ _ n   v _ _ age   enj _ _

p _ _ nt   p _ _ son   cowb _ _

2 Cross out the word in each row that does not have the same sound as the first word.

toy	boy	loose	joy
voice	boil	point	paint
enjoy	coy	toy	buy

3 Put a check (✔) in the box next to the word that names the picture.

☐ flown

☐ flower

☐ crow

☐ cow

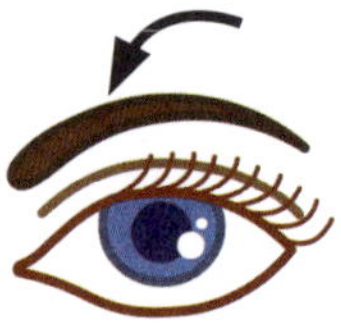

☐ eyebrow

☐ elbow

☐ growl

☐ grown

Time Filler:
Draw a silly picture of a cow. Give her a grumpy frown and big eyebrows. Label each part of your picture with the correct word: "cow," "frown," and "eyebrows."

(4) Complete each picture's name with the letters **oi** or **oy**.

b _ _

s _ _ l

c _ _ n

c _ _ l

(5) Help Busy Bee find his way to Fuzzy Bee. Color in the hexagons that have words with the sound you hear in "how."

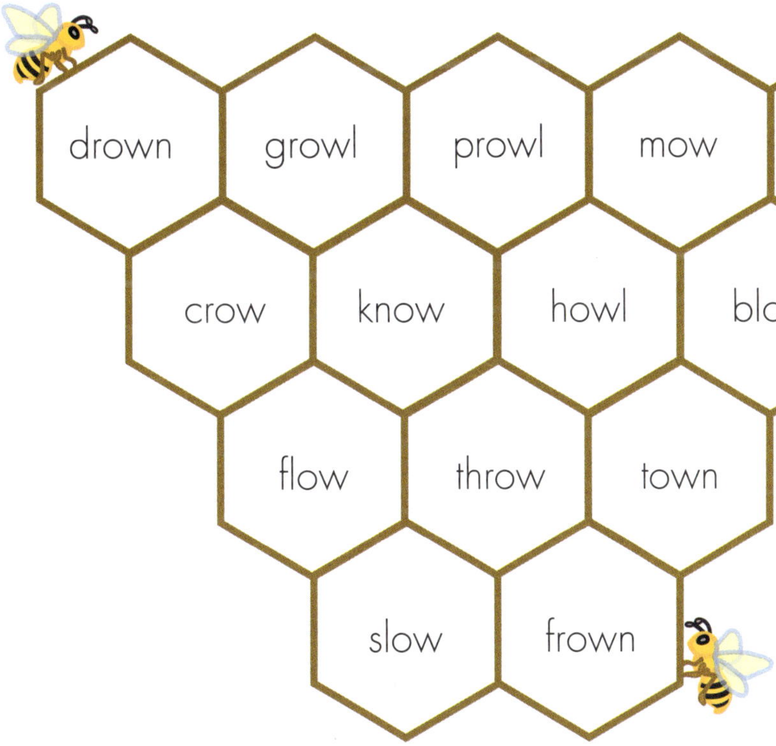

Vowels with **r**

The letter **r** can team up with each vowel and change the vowel's sound. Listen to the sounds you hear in the words "far," "her," "circus," "horn," and "burn."

1 Choose the letter team that completes each picture's name.

ur/er

t__tle

or/ir

sh__t

er/ir

f__n

ar/ir

sk__t

ar/er

sh__k

ar/er

y__n

2 Use **ar**, **er**, **or**, **ir**, and **ur** to complete the words. Then draw lines to match the words with the same **r** team.

f__k	moth__
g__m	st__m
h__l	m__k
h__m	c__l
th__ty	b__thday

Time Filler:
Name the r team word for each of these clues: between second and fourth; it shines in the night sky; you use it to eat; a group of cows.

3 Circle the picture in each row whose name includes the same **r** sound as the first picture. Write the name on the dotted line.

shorts

bird

bear

horse

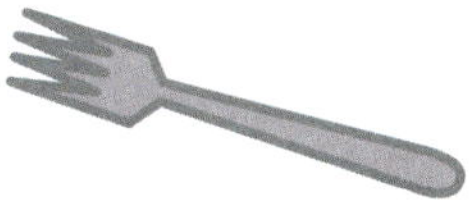

Letter Blends

Letters can blend together to make one sound. The blends **sn**, **sp**, and **squ** can be found at the beginning of words. The blends **lf**, **lt**, and **nch** can be found at the end of words.

1. Choose the correct word to complete each sentence.

Can you teach me how to read and .... ?	spell/space
I had a .... before lunch today.	snap/snack
Have you ever seen a white .... ?	squirrel/squirm
Mary .... ice cream on her dress.	spice/spilled
When you ...., please cover your mouth.	snuggle/sneeze

2. Add the letters **squ** to complete each word. Then circle the word that rhymes with "please" and draw a rectangle around the word that names a shape.

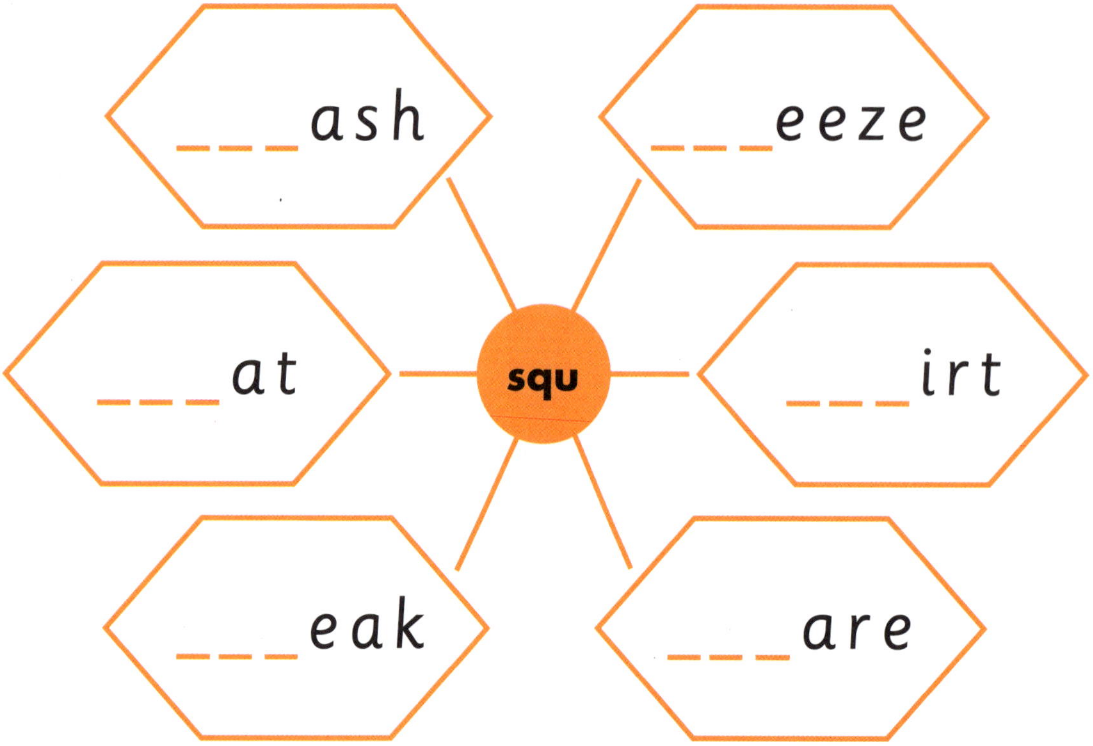

Time Filler:
Go through an old magazine and look for pictures of things whose names either begin with sn or sp or end with lf or lt. See if you can find two or three of each.

3 Draw a line from each picture to the blend at the end of its name.

elf

branch

salt

nch **lt** **lf**

shelf

bench

belt

4 Find the words from the box in the word search below.

melt lunch myself flow adult

f	l	o	w	f	o
m	y	s	e	l	f
e	b	q	u	n	t
l	u	n	c	h	h
t	a	d	u	l	t

Syllables

Syllables are parts of words. Each syllable has a vowel. When a consonant follows a vowel, it often ends the first syllable.

1) Write the number of syllables you hear for each word below.

dragon ....

visit ....

planet ....

men ....

sit ....

pizza ....

2) Place a dot to separate each syllable in the words below.

minute

river

curly

finish

fraction

journey

never

complain

Time Filler:
You can become good at spelling by learning to spell many words one syllable at a time. Say the first syllable and then write it down. Do the same for the next syllable and so on.

3 Color the box yellow if the word has one syllable.
Color the box red if the word has two syllables.
Color the box blue if the word has three syllables.

had	picnic	fantastic	false
dentist	cap	sit	window
pencil	contest	basket	kangaroo

4 Choose the correct word from the box to complete each sentence. Then write the number of syllables in the word on the line.

chimpanzee fancy ribbon lock

Mary wore a .... dress to the party. ....

I saw a .... at the wildlife park. ....

The present was wrapped with a ....

Be sure to .... the door when you leave. ....

5 Place a dot to separate each syllable in the words below.

b i r t h d a y　　c a p t a i n
h i d d e n　　p i c n i c
g e n e r a l　　i n s t e a d

More Syllables

Some beginning syllables end in a vowel. That vowel makes a long sound.

1) Write the number of syllables there are in each word below.

recycle	....	reuse	....
begin	....	even	....
pilot	....	student	....
music	....	cafeteria	....

2) Write the number of syllables for each word on the line. Then draw a line from the word to its picture.

.... bicycle

.... baker

.... coconut

.... elephant

Time Filler:
Write down ten two-syllable words. Then separate them into two lists: those whose first syllable has a short vowel sound, such as "kitten," and those whose first syllable has a long vowel sound, such as "tiger."

3. Separate each word's syllables by writing them in each column.

Words	Syllables			
delivery				
electric				
baby				
motor				
super				
tomato				

4. Read the words below. Put a dot to separate each syllable in each word. Then read the instructions that follow.

paper secret

volcano below

potato relax

Circle the word that means "to chill out."
Draw a rectangle around the word that names a vegetable.

Double Consonants

In some words, consonants are doubled after a short vowel sound.

1 Find these words with double consonants in the word search.

muddy daddy marry call rabbit button

b	y	m	s	l	e	r
u	p	u	p	p	m	a
t	a	d	a	d	a	b
t	d	d	c	h	r	b
o	s	y	e	i	r	i
n	d	a	d	d	y	t
c	a	l	l	g	q	m

2 Complete each word by doubling either the letter **l** or **n**.

wi_ _ te_ _is

fe_ _ do_ _

ru_ _y si_ _y

di_ _er ba_ _

Time Filler:
Can you think of words that include double c, g, and z? Try to write down three of each. Which consonants do you never see doubled up in words?

3 Draw a line to match each picture to its name.

rabbit

puppy

raccoon

hippo

squirrel

kitten

4 Choose the correctly spelled word to complete each sentence.

I use two .... when I go to sleep. pilows/pillows

We all went to a .... show yesterday. puppet/pupet

The dog .... the meat on the table. snift/sniffed

Jen had .... at her friend's house last night. diner/dinner

I got lost because I had the wrong .... address/adress

Compound Words

Some words are made by putting two different words together.

1) Look at each pair of pictures. You can make a compound word by joining their names together. Choose the correct compound word from the box and write it on the dotted line.

eyeball	horseshoe	doorbell	butterfly

....

....

....

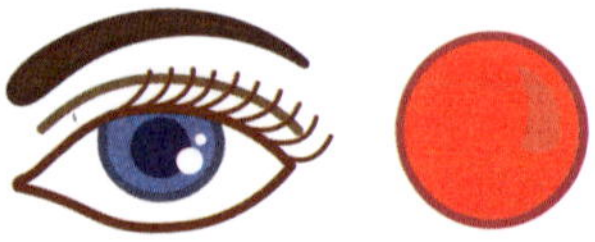

....

2) What word can you add to each of these groups of words to make a compound word? Write that word on the line.

bed lunch day

....

skate chalk clip

....

base basket volley

....

blue straw black

....

Time Filler:
See how many compound words you can make that include one of these words: "ball," "self," "house," "brush," and "fire."

3) Help the children reach their grandfather's barn. Color each stone that has a compound word.

bulldog

juice

drive

football

dinner

learn

cookbook

house

back

bedroom

4) Read each compound word. Write the two words that make up the compound word.

grapefruit = ... + ...
playground = ... + ...
fingernail = ... + ...

Plural Endings

Plural words name more than one of something. We write plural spellings in different ways.

1 We add **s** to most nouns to make them plural. We add **es** to nouns that end in **s**, **x**, **z**, **ch**, or **sh**. Based on these rules, write **s** or **es** at the end of the words below.

coin__ class__

patch__ whale__

flower__ pencil__

2 When forming the plural of words ending in **f** or **fe**, we change the **f** or **fe** to **v** and then add **es**. Now write the correct plural form for each word below.

half	life	loaf ....
knife	calf	wolf ....

Time Filler:
Write a list of all the different ways that you have learned to make plurals. Then think of one example for each way you have listed.

3 If a word ends in a consonant and **y**, we drop the **y** and add **ies**. Look at each pair of words below. Circle the correct spelling of the plural form.

cherries / cherryes   daisies / daisyz

ladys / ladies   pennies / pennyes

babys / babies   ponies / ponys

4 There are some exceptions to the rules for forming plurals. Read the words below and write their plurals. Observe how different they are from the singular forms.

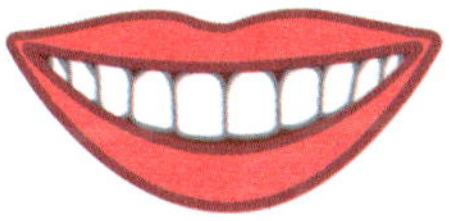

tooth ....

mouse ....

child ....

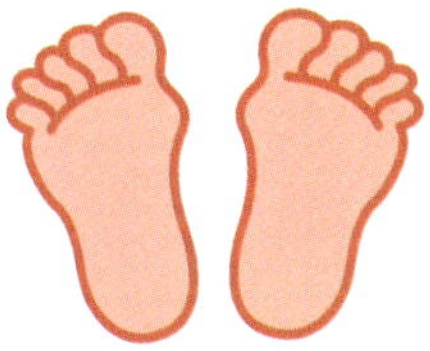

foot ....

Prefix Power

A prefix is a set of letters that is added to the beginning of a word to change its meaning.

1. The prefix **pre** added to a word can mean "before." The prefix **un** added to a word can mean "not." Add **un** or **pre** to the words below to make new words.

___happy ___kind ___view
___fair ___school ___like

2. The prefix **non** added to a word can mean "without." The prefix **bi** added to a word can mean "two." Sort the words from the box under the two headings **non** and **bi** to make new words.

fiction monthly cycle sense weekly stop

non	**bi**
....	....
....	....
....	....

3. The prefix **sub** added to a word can mean "under." Draw a line from each word to its meaning.

subzero — vehicle for under the sea
submerge — put under water
submarine — under zero

Time Filler:
Give yourself three minutes. How many words with prefixes can you say in that time?

4 The prefix **dis** added to a word can mean "the opposite of." Check (✔) the box with the correct meaning for each word below.

dislike
- to not like ☐
- to not dive ☐

disobey
- to not care ☐
- to not obey ☐

dishonest
- without honor ☐
- without honesty ☐

disappear
- to not appear ☐
- to not hear ☐

5 Choose words from the box to complete each sentence.

mistake	unavailable	returned	unable

Today, I .... to the shoe store.

But I was .... to find the green shoes I saw last week.

The clerk told me that they were now ....

It was a .... not to buy them earlier.

Useful Word List 2

Read each column of words. Then cover the words up one by one and write them. Then move on to the next column.

describe ....

ache ....

knife ....

comb ....

autumn ....

fierce ....

banquet ....

equal ....

journey ....

burrow ....

champion ....

guitar ....

liquid ....

collar ....

biscuit ....

aloud ....

majesty ....

design ....

invisible ....

gasp ....

Time Filler:
Make sentences using the words here. Keep coming back to this list to check that you still know the spellings of these useful words.

bulb	calm ....
faint	jungle ....
ceiling	aim ....
bait	desert ....
fright	knight ....
lamb	label ....
foam	envelope ....
ghost	level ....
drift	eagle ....
handle	museum ....

Suffixes

A suffix is a set of letters that is added to the end of a word to change its meaning.

1 The suffix **able** added to a word can mean "able to."
The suffix **less** added to a word can mean "without."
Draw a line to match each word to its meaning.

hopeless	able to be washed
enjoyable	without spots
washable	without hope
spotless	able to be enjoyed

2 The suffix **ness** added to a word can mean "a state of being." The suffix **ment** added to a word can mean "an act or happening." The suffix **ful** added to a word can mean "full of." Write the words from the box under the suffixes **ment**, **ness**, or **ful**.

amuse fear kind happy treat
sad joy pay cheer

ment	ness	ful
....	....	....
....	....	....
....	....	....

Time Filler:
Draw a circle and divide it into four sections. Write a word with the suffix able in each section. Repeat the activity with the suffixes ment and ful.

3 The suffix **est** added to a word can mean "most." Complete each set by writing the third word.

close	closer	....	happy	happier	....
soft	softer	....	light	lighter	....

4 Match each description to the word it describes. Write the number of the word next to the correct letter. To check your answers, add the numbers in each column and row. They should be the same!

A. full of grace	1. happiness
B. state of being dark	2. enjoyment
C. act of enjoying	3. treatment
D. act of treating	4. graceful
E. full of care	5. careful
F. able to be washed	6. luckiest
G. able to agree	7. washable
H. state of being happy	8. agreeable
I. most lucky	9. darkness

A.	B.	C. ....
D.	E.	F. ....
G.	H.	I. ....

Homophones

Words that sound the same but have different meanings and often different spellings are called homophones.

1 Choose the correct word to complete each sentence.

The players .... the best bats and balls. chews/choose

.... always determined to win. There/They're

You'll never .... them give up. sea/see

They always keep their .... on the ball. eye/I

2 In each row, find the pairs of words and phrases that go together. Color the boxes with those pairs in each row the same color.

sent	an odor	posted	scent
piece of wood	not interested	bored	board
hair	hare	covers the scalp	animal like a rabbit
not strong	week	weak	seven days
part of a plant	flower	finely ground grain	flour
heel	back part of foot	to get better	heal

Time Filler:
Choose three pairs of homophones to illustrate. Draw your own pictures or cut them from magazines.

3 Circle the homophones in each sentence.

We are allowed to speak aloud.

We know that no other team is like ours.

John threw the ball a long way through the air.

He rose from his seat to give the speaker a rose.

4 Write a homophone for each word below.

blew ....

peace ....

write ....

male ....

sum ....

Antonyms

Words that mean the opposite of each other are called antonyms.

1) Draw a line from each word to its antonym.

dirty

old

smile

clean

young

frown

2) Look at the pictures of the food items and read their descriptions. Write an antonym for the underlined word.

<u>sour</u> juice

....

<u>straight</u> fries

....

<u>thin</u> smoothie

....

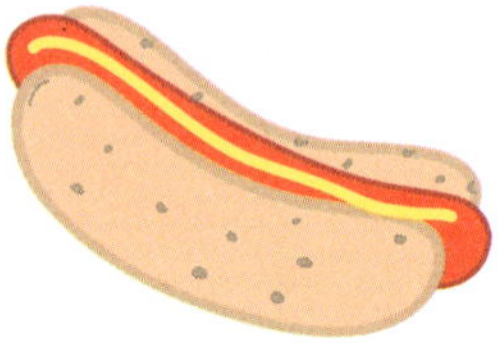
<u>worst</u> hot dog

....

Time Filler:
Choose a category such as position words, like "on," or describing words, like "hot." How quickly can you name some of those category words and their opposites?

3 Circle the antonym for the underlined word in each sentence below.

Someone had left the door open, but Jon wanted it shut.

We got to the fair early and stayed until late that night.

We crossed the bridge over the river and took the tunnel under the road.

4 Write the antonym for the underlined word in each sentence below.

Dad has already mowed the upper lawn and is now mowing the .... part.

Jan is not in front of me but is somewhere .... me.

If you cannot fix my bike, it will .... my heart.

My brother likes to eat cold pizza, but I prefer .... pizza.

My dog is sad when he is alone, but he is .... when I play with him.

Synonyms

Words that have the same or almost the same meaning are called synonyms.

1 For each sentence, write a word from the box that is the synonym for the underlined word.

relax	prepare	glance	heats

Mother will make dinner soon. ....

The sun warms the ground. ....

Take a look at that large dog. ....

Let's rest before we go out again. ....

2 Choose two words that are synonyms from the word box. Then write them in pairs below.

injured	choose	tired	weary	hurt	select

....	....	....
....	....	....

3 Circle the synonym for the underlined word in each sentence below.

Tom saw a small purple stone in the little pond.

The present was beautifully wrapped at the gift shop.

Time Filler:
Can you think of a synonym for each of these words: "tasty," "dinner," "pair," "stone," and "store"? Can you think of an antonym for each of these words: "heavy," "true," "silent," "small," and "work"?

4) Help Patrick the pink rabbit hop his way through the maze to reach the tasty carrots. Color only the boxes that have true statements.

A synonym for "answer" is "reply."

Another word for "city" is "country."

Another word for "idea" is "thought."

A synonym for "still" is "silent."

The opposite of "sea" is "ocean."

An antonym for "above" is "below."

Another word for "near" is "far."

A synonym for "happy" is "glad."

An antonym for "tiny" is "small."

An antonym for "find" is "lose."

An antonym for "job" is "work."

Another word for "happy" is "sad."

Another word for "border" is "edge."

The opposite of "find" is "locate."

The antonym for "child" is "adult."

Verb Endings

The letters **ed** or **ied** can be added to verbs to show that something happened in the past. The letters **ing** can be added to verbs to show something is happening now.

1 Look at each word below. Drop the verb ending for each and write the root word (infinitive) on the line.

explored ....

walked ....

painting ....

studied ....

2 Find the verb in each sentence. Circle its **ing** or **ed** ending.

Jan slipped on the icy sidewalk.

Joe planned a trip to California.

Are you going to the beach now?

Jake finally finished his homework at 7 o'clock.

I am drawing a picture for my art class.

Time Filler:
Look quickly through one page of a story or newspaper article. Make a note of the different verb endings that you see.

3 Color the six boxes that have correctly spelled verbs.

learning	takeing	stopping	tradeing
carrying	singging	humming	runing
countting	flying	choping	spending

Write the correct spelling for the other six words below.

....

....

4 Add **ed** to each root word below. **Remember:** you may have to double some consonants first!

watch .... start .... drop ....

want .... slap .... crash ....

5 Add **ied** to each root word below. **Remember:** drop the **y** first!

carry .... worry ....

cry .... try ....

hurry .... marry ....

The Letters **c** and **g**

The letters **c** and **g** can be pronounced differently depending on the word. For example: "car" or "circle" for the letter **c**; "goat" or "gentle" for the letter **g**.

1. Find the word in each row that is spelled correctly. Circle the word and say it aloud.

ciicle	cyycle	cycle
page	paage	pag
coyn	coin	coiin

2. Choose the correct word to complete each sentence below.

I picked the salad with .... selery/celery

She likes a lot of .... in her drink. ice/ize

Please give me a .... helping. large/lurge

They will form the .... govenment/government

3. Circle the incorrectly spelled word in each row below.

caught	centur	coach
jentle	giant	game
going	giive	gang

Time Filler:
How many things in your kitchen have names beginning with the letter c or g? Look for them. How do you pronounce and spell each item?

4) Color the box if the word in it is spelled correctly. Put an **X** on the incorrectly spelled word. Then write the correct words below.

frog	cake	carry	genaral
cilk	jinjer	kave	dance

....

5) Draw a line from the picture to its name only if it is spelled correctly.

jiraffe caje juice dog coin face

Which Word?

Nouns name a person, place, or thing. Verbs name an action. Adjectives describe a person, place, or thing.

1 Read each sentence. Find the one word that is spelled incorrectly in the sentence. Underline it and then write it correctly on the line.

I am a hapy person. ....

They are runing quickly ....

Tom told a funy joke. ....

Mary is rideing a bike. ....

2 Choose the correctly spelled verb, or action word, to complete each sentence.

We ran to the store to .... ice cream. by/buy

His father .... home after the game. droove/drove

Jim .... cookies for the school sale. baked/bakt

Joan liked to fish and .... in the stream. waade/wade

3 Write your own adjective, or describing word, to complete each sentence. Use a dictionary to check the spelling.

Mom baked a .... birthday cake for me.

The cheese sandwiches were very ....

Sally took a .... trip to the zoo.

The eagle had .... wings.

Time Filler:
Think of more naming, action, or describing words and make a list for each type. Be sure to spell them correctly. Use a dictionary if you need help with their spellings.

4 Read the ten naming words, or nouns, in the box and then find them in the word search.

pavement		key	library
crab	drum	towel	fuzz
carrot		wheat	river

p	x	c	c	a	r	r	o	t
a	o	p	b	a	i	f	l	k
v	d	r	u	m	v	u	i	g
e	d	a	h	r	e	z	b	e
m	k	e	y	t	r	z	r	t
e	k	d	s	x	c	o	a	o
n	i	u	x	w	r	d	r	w
t	q	z	p	r	a	k	y	e
w	h	e	a	t	b	n	m	l

Sentence Sense

Knowing how to spell words and use them correctly will help improve your reading and writing skills.

1. Read each sentence below. Circle the incorrectly spelled word. Then write it correctly on the line.

We are having our schull picnic tomorrow. ....

Where is the picnic going to be helled? ....

What are you takeing to the picnic? ....

I am worryed about what I should take. ....

Maybe I will take a lemin cake. ....

Let's hope it doesn't rayne tomorrow. ....

Time Filler:
Write three sentences. Use the word "world" in one of them. Use different synonyms for "world" in the other two sentences.

2 When you write sentences, you use **who**, **when**, and **where** words. Correct the spelling for each word in the box and then write it under one of the three headings.

wryter	artest	toodae	tommorrow	nerse
danser	aftre	citie	teecher	beforr
purson	libarry	sisstur	Febuary	offiss
iland	dezert	parc	Sonday	peeple
Fryday	yustrday	outdores	hoam	unkle
skool	Oggust	faather	muzeam	evrydae

Who	When	Where
....	....	....
....	....	....
....	....	....
....	....	....
....	....	....
....	....	....
....	....	....
....	....	....
....	....	....
....	....	....

Spelling Sense

Knowing the spellings and meanings of words helps you read accurately.

Read the story below and then answer the questions that follow.

Wonderful Trees

Trees are wonderful. They help our Earth and all living things. Do you no how they help?

Trees help klean our air. They take in a harmful gas from the air and use it to make their own food. The trees use the fod. The leaves give off a clean gas for people to breathe.

Trees do many other helpful things. Their leaves give us shade from the sun. Trees give workers wood to build houses and other things. Some parts of a tree are used to make the paper we write on.

Trees also give animals homes. Woodpeckers use holes in trees to make nests for their babies. Squirrels build nests high in the branches of trees. They store nuts in tree holes and eat them during the cold winter when food is hard to find. Owls use twigs from trees to make their nests. Insects such as beetles live on or under the bark of trees. A mother fox will sometimes use a hollow tree trunk as a den for her cubs.

Trees do so many things for our world. What would we do without them?

Time Filler:
Make a list of the names of animals included in the story below using the correct spelling. Then write the names of two parts of a tree you read about. Spell them correctly.

1. Find the word in line 2 that is spelled incorrectly. Correct it here.

....

2. Find the incorrectly spelled word in line 3. Write the correct spelling here.

....

3. Look at line 4. Find the word to which you need to add another **o** to correct its spelling. Write it correctly here.

....

4. Which of these is the correct spelling of the word? Circle it.

shayd shade shede

5. The word "nests" is in the story. Write a rhyming word for it.

....

6. "Sometimes" is made up of two words. Think of another word that is made up of two words. Write it here.

....

Useful Word List 3

Read each column of words. Then cover the words up one by one and write them. Then move on to the next column.

could	....	Monday	....
should	....	Tuesday	....
would	....	Wednesday	....
very	....	Thursday	....
every	....	Friday	....
other	....	Saturday	....
another	....	Sunday	....
because	....	today	....
open	....	tomorrow	....
close	....	yesterday	....

Time Filler:
Make sentences using the words here. Keep coming back to this list to check that you still know the spellings of these useful words.

January ....

February ....

March ....

April ....

May ....

June ....

July ....

August ....

September ....

October ....

November ....

December ....

month ....

year ....

school ....

rain ....

cloud ....

snow ....

wind ....

weather ....

Answers:

04–05 Long Vowel Sounds
06–07 Short Vowel Sounds

4

1 Add the missing vowel (**a**, **e**, **i**, **o**, or **u**) to complete each word.

juice meat cake

baby potato knife

2 Draw lines to match the pairs of words that have the same vowel sound.

soap flute size cape leap

light rope peek cube bait

3 Circle the two words with long vowel sounds in each sentence.

Dan (made) an error in the (game).

Ann (gave) Jon (five) pens.

The (paint) was (blue).

5

4 Look at each picture and read the words with long vowel sounds below. Then circle the word that names the picture.

pine	hide	mile
pipe	(hive)	(mice)
(peach)	high	pile

5 Color the pieces of the pie that have long vowel words.

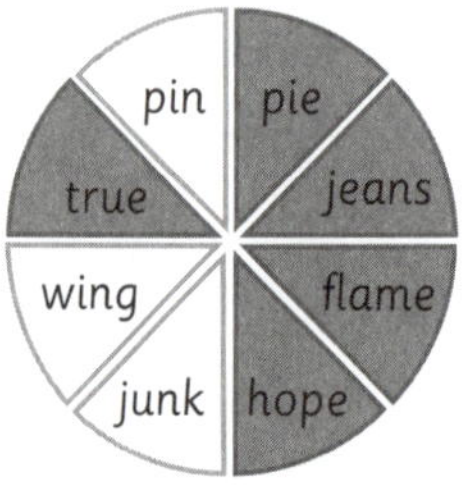

Let your child say aloud the names of the days of the week and the months of the year. Ask him or her which of these names contain long vowel sounds.

6

1 Read the two words in each row aloud. Listen to the sound of the letters in bold. Choose a word from the box with the same vowel sound.

lunch jog mad net dig

kn**o**b, h**o**t ....jog........

l**u**ck, d**u**st ....lunch........

m**a**gic, l**a**dder ....mad........

d**i**nner, d**i**p ....dig........

p**e**t, t**e**n ....net........

2 Choose a short vowel word from the box to answer each clue.

dog neck bell red sun duck ball

an animal that barks ....dog........

the name of a color ....red........

it holds your head up ....neck........

something that rings ....bell........

it shines brightly in the sky ....sun........

an animal that quacks ....duck........

a round toy that is thrown, kicked, or hit ....ball........

7

3 Read the six short vowel words in the box. Now look in the word search for those words. Draw a circle around each one.

mess frog fox mix rush swam

s	w	a	m	q	n
f	r	o	g	a	l
o	l	m	i	x	e
x	r	e	n	b	p
r	u	s	h	c	h
t	k	s	d	e	t

4 Sort the words from the box under the correct heading.

dream patch train cone wish jet

Long vowel words	Short vowel words
dream	patch
train	wish
cone	jet

Write these short vowel words on index cards: "black," "cat," "deck," "pen," "hit," "think," "top," "shock," "push," and "pull." Mix them up and place them facedown on a table. Help your child play a memory game using the index cards by matching up the five pairs with the same vowel sound.

Answers:

08–09 The Letter **y**

10–11 The Long **a** Letter Teams

8

9

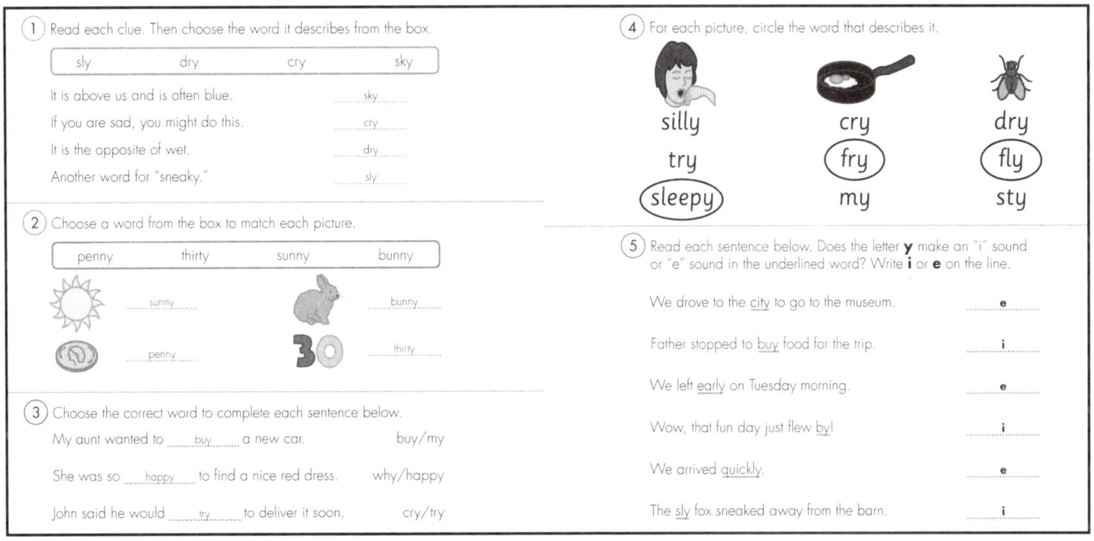

1) Read each clue. Then choose the word it describes from the box.

sly dry cry sky

It is above us and is often blue. sky

If you are sad, you might do this. cry

It is the opposite of wet. dry

Another word for "sneaky." sly

2) Choose a word from the box to match each picture.

penny thirty sunny bunny

sunny

bunny

penny

thirty

3) Choose the correct word to complete each sentence below.

My aunt wanted to buy a new car. buy/my

She was so happy to find a nice red dress. why/happy

John said he would try to deliver it soon. cry/try

4) For each picture, circle the word that describes it.

silly / try / (sleepy)

cry / (fry) / my

dry / (fly) / sty

5) Read each sentence below. Does the letter **y** make an "i" sound or "e" sound in the underlined word? Write **i** or **e** on the line.

We drove to the city to go to the museum. e

Father stopped to buy food for the trip. i

We left early on Tuesday morning. e

Wow, that fun day just flew by! i

We arrived quickly. e

The sly fox sneaked away from the barn. i

Write 10 one- or two-syllable words ending in **y** on separate index cards. Let your child read each word aloud and then sort them into two piles: **y** with the long **e** sound and **y** with the long **i** sound. For extra fun, ask your child to make a sentence with each word.

10

11

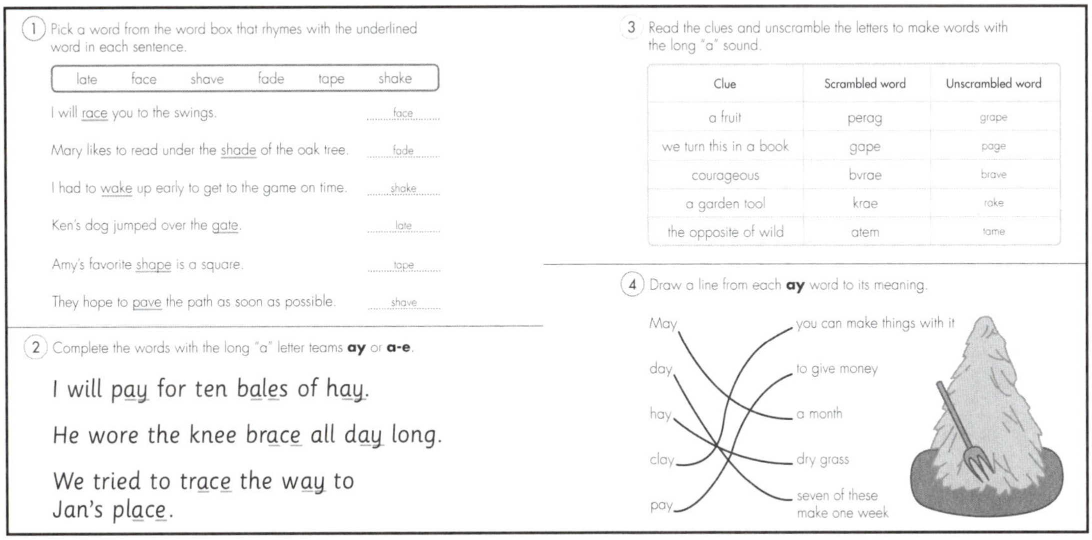

1) Pick a word from the word box that rhymes with the underlined word in each sentence.

late face shave fade tape shake

I will race you to the swings. face

Mary likes to read under the shade of the oak tree. fade

I had to wake up early to get to the game on time. shake

Ken's dog jumped over the gate. late

Amy's favorite shape is a square. tape

They hope to pave the path as soon as possible. shave

2) Complete the words with the long "a" letter teams **ay** or **a-e**.

I will pay for ten bales of hay.

He wore the knee brace all day long.

We tried to trace the way to Jan's place.

3) Read the clues and unscramble the letters to make words with the long "a" sound.

Clue	Scrambled word	Unscrambled word
a fruit	perag	grape
we turn this in a book	gape	page
courageous	bvrae	brave
a garden tool	krae	rake
the opposite of wild	atem	tame

4) Draw a line from each **ay** word to its meaning.

May — you can make things with it

day — to give money

hay — a month

clay — dry grass

pay — seven of these make one week

Encourage your child to write simple sentences or even a poem using either **ay** or **a-e** words. Some words he or she could use are "day," "way," "place," "face," "say," "care," and "dare."

Answers:

12–13 The Long **e** Vowel Teams

14–15 The Long **i** Letter Teams

12

1) Help Queen Colleen reach her peaches! Add **ee** or **ea** to each stone to make a word. If you cannot make a real word, cross out the stone. Color the stones with real words to show the queen's path.

2) Use the letters of the alphabet to make rhyming **ee** and **ea** words.
a b c d e f g h i j k l m n o p q r s t u v w x y z
Answers may vary.

teach	reach	bee	see
team	beam	clean	bean
cheek	seek	sheep	deep

13

3) Find and circle **ee** and **ea** words in each sentence below.

Last (week) I saw a hive of (bees) by the (stream).

"The (heat) has made me (feel) (weak)," said (Jean).

The (screen) (seems) to be torn in at (least) (three) places.

4) Complete each picture's name with either the **ee** or **ea** vowel team.

sheep

meet

weep

seat

feet

leap

Write sentences containing **ee** and **ea** words that are spelled incorrectly. Encourage your child to read each sentence, note any misspelled words, and write them correctly.

14

1) Pick a word from the box to complete each sentence.

right knife bright fries dried

It was a windy day, so the clothes on the line quickly dried.

The sun was bright and warm when we played outside.

The sharp knife sliced the bread easily.

I had the best fries I have ever tasted yesterday.

Sean checked to see if he had the right answer.

2) The vowel team **ie** doesn't always make the long "i" sound. Sometimes it makes the long "e" sound. Read the first word in each row. Then circle the word in the row that has the same long "i" sound.

fried	chief	(lie)
life	(tries)	field
high	niece	(ties)
night	(sigh)	brief

15

3) Read the words in the grid below. Color the boxes that include words with the long "i" sound.

pie	yield	tight	belief
shield	sight	grief	high
cookie	die	cries	chief

4) Read the two words under each picture. Then circle the word that names the picture.

(flies) fight

(fried) tie

tight (light)

5) Unscramble the letters to make words with the **igh** or **ie** letter teams.

sskei	timhg	lfgiht
skies	might	flight
ipe	gihh	ite
pie	high	tie

Say aloud some **igh** and **ie** words to your child, one at a time. Let him or her record each word in a column: one labeled **igh** and the other labeled **ie**.

Answers:

16–17 The Long **o** Letter Teams

18–19 The Long **u** Vowel Teams

20–21 Useful Word List 1, see p. 80

16

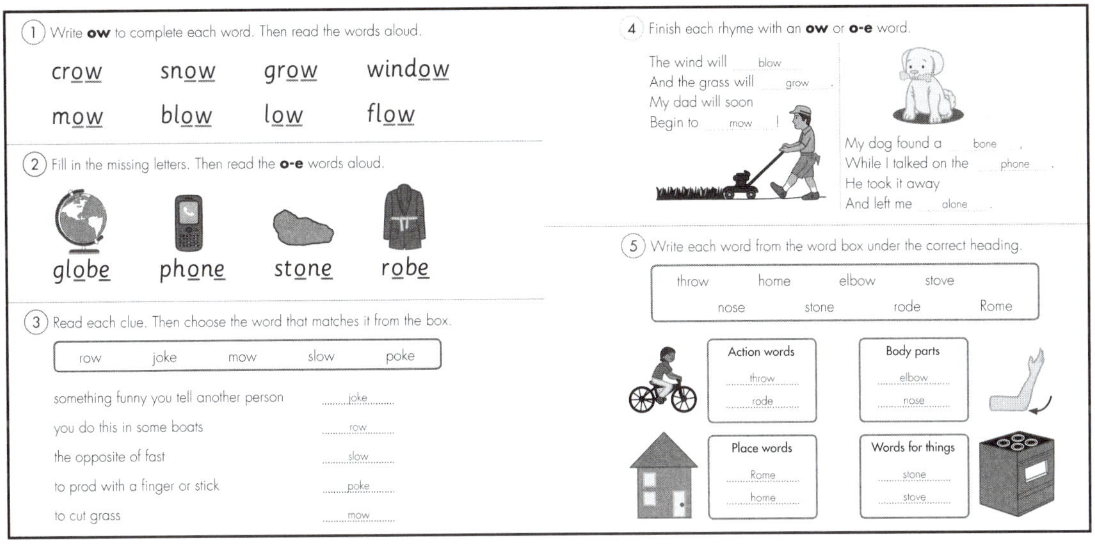
1 Write **ow** to complete each word. Then read the words aloud.

crow snow grow window

mow blow low flow

2 Fill in the missing letters. Then read the **o-e** words aloud.

globe phone stone robe

3 Read each clue. Then choose the word that matches it from the box.

row joke mow slow poke

something funny you tell another person joke

you do this in some boats row

the opposite of fast slow

to prod with a finger or stick poke

to cut grass mow

4 Finish each rhyme with an **ow** or **o-e** word.

The wind will blow

And the grass will grow.

My dad will soon

Begin to mow!

My dog found a bone,

While I talked on the phone.

He took it away

And left me alone.

5 Write each word from the word box under the correct heading.

throw home elbow stove nose stone rode Rome

Action words	Body parts	Place words	Words for things
throw	elbow	Rome	stone
rode	nose	home	stove

17

With your child, look through newspapers and magazines for long **o** words spelled either with **ow** or **o-e**. Cut them out and glue them onto a piece of paper, making a list for each type of spelling. Invite your child to review them frequently.

18

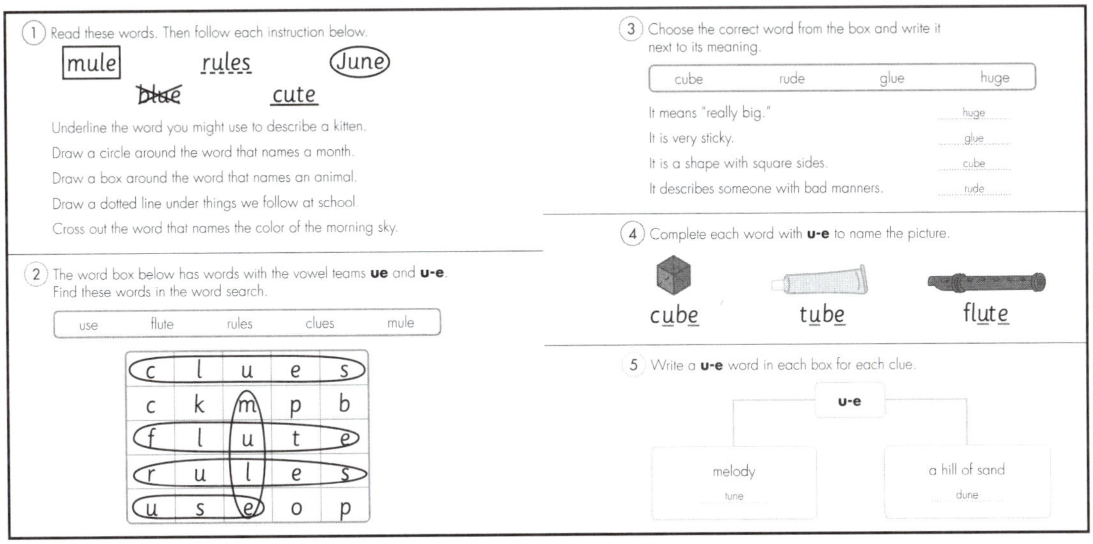
1 Read these words. Then follow each instruction below.

mule rules June

~~blue~~ cute

Underline the word you might use to describe a kitten.

Draw a circle around the word that names a month.

Draw a box around the word that names an animal.

Draw a dotted line under things we follow at school.

Cross out the word that names the color of the morning sky.

2 The word box below has words with the vowel teams **ue** and **u-e**. Find these words in the word search.

use flute rules clues mule

c	l	u	e	s
c	k	m	p	b
f	l	u	t	e
r	u	l	e	s
u	s	e	o	p

3 Choose the correct word from the box and write it next to its meaning.

cube rude glue huge

It means "really big." huge

It is very sticky. glue

It is a shape with square sides. cube

It describes someone with bad manners. rude

4 Complete each word with **u-e** to name the picture.

cube tube flute

5 Write a **u-e** word in each box for each clue.

u-e

melody tune

a hill of sand dune

19

Write three **u-e** words on index cards. One of them should not rhyme with the other two. Let your child read the words and decide which one does not rhyme. For example, the words may be "cute," "mule," and "chute."

Answers:

22–23 The **oo** Vowel Team

24–25 Other Vowel Sounds

22

(1) Say each word in the box aloud. Then write it under the correct heading based on the sound it makes.

loose tooth look proof book hood

"oo" as in "soon"	"oo" as in "foot"
tooth	look
proof	hood
loose	book

(2) Read each sentence. If the underlined word has the "oo" sound of "soon," write an **s** on the line. If it has the "oo" sound of "foot," write an **f** on the line.

The flowers began to bloom in the garden. s

Please give me a scoop of chocolate ice cream. s

Jenny is the best cook in her family. f

His father shook the rug to get rid of the dust. f

Tina chopped some wood for her grandmother. f

Faye was so sick she could not leave her room. s

23

(3) Some words are in the wrong place! Cross out the words that do not have the "oo" sound of "foot" on the foot. Cross out the words that do not have "oo" sound of "moon" on the moon.

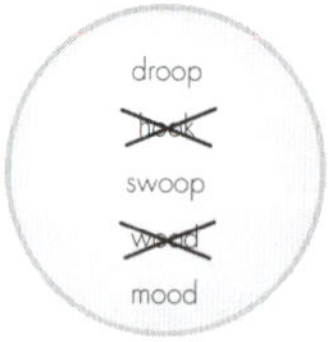

(4) Write three words for each **oo** spelling pattern: **oon**, **ool**, and **ook**. Hint: they're the sounds you hear in "soon," "cool," and "look."

Answers may vary.

soon	cool	look
noon	school	hook
spoon	tool	brook
baboon	drool	cook

Create sentences in which your child uses an **oo** word. For example: Her foot is on the grass.

After that, ask him or her to say whether the **oo** word has a "moon" or "wood" sound.

24

(1) Sort the words from the box into the letter teams for **aw**, **al**, and **au** words.

shawl taught fawn sauce halt caught salt yawn false

aw	**al**	**au**
shawl	halt	caught
fawn	salt	sauce
yawn	false	taught

(2) Use the words from the box to complete each sentence. Note the vowel sounds.

bawl seesaw dawn launch crawled paused

To send up a rocket is to launch it.

The children enjoyed playing on the seesaw.

The baby started to bawl noisily at bedtime.

At dawn, we went out for a long hike.

She paused before she finished speaking.

The spider crawled across its web.

25

(3) Complete the words in each sentence below. Then find the words in the word search and circle them.

My dog is smaller than your cat!

She caught the ball quickly.

Jon helped his father haul wood.

The cat has sharp claws.

c	a	u	g	h	t	e	h
l	p	l	w	s	y	b	a
a	h	b	a	l	l	n	u
w	r	w	n	b	p	t	l
s	s	m	a	l	l	e	r

(4) Use the alphabet to find a rhyming word for each word below.

a b c d e f g h i j k l m n o p q r s t u v w x y z

Answers may vary.

law saw ball tall

fawn lawn raw jaw

Provide word cards with the letter team **aw** or **au** missing from the word. Let your child write in the correct letters to complete the word and then read it aloud. Here are some words to get you started: "cauldron," "bawl," "straw," "laundry," and "fault."

Answers:

26–27 More Vowel Sounds

28–29 Vowels with r

26

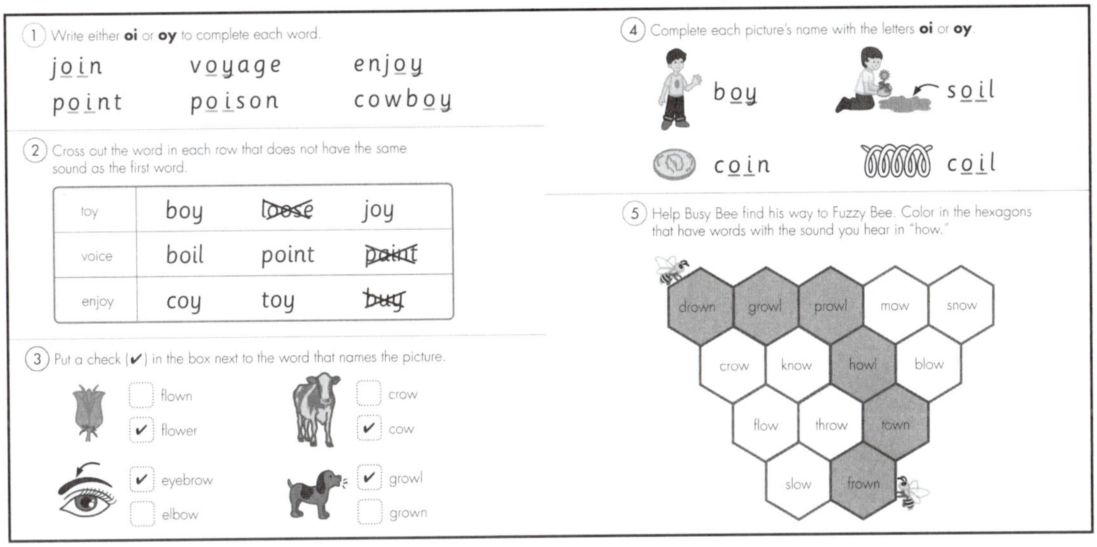

27

Prepare index cards with **ow** words written on them. Some of the words should have the "now" sound while others have the long "o" sound, as in "low." Place them facedown. Let your child turn one over and read it. If he or she gets the sound correct, give him or her a point. Repeat with various other words until your child has the maximum number of points possible.

28

29

Help your child make silly sentences using **r** team words, such as "The guard drove his car very far in the tar" or "The third bird tried to stir the dirt."

Answers:

30–31 Letter Blends

32–33 Syllables

30

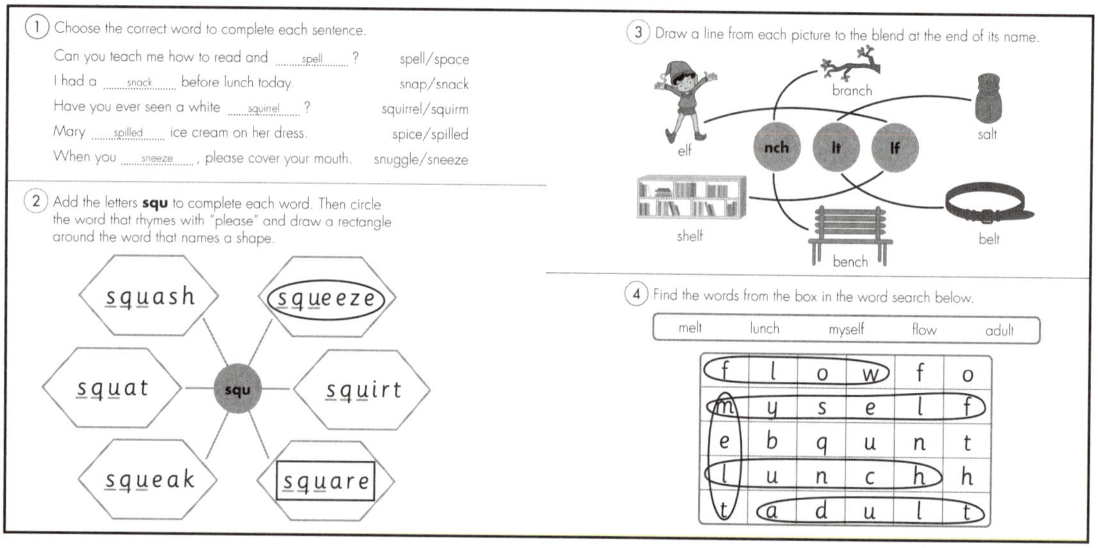

1 Choose the correct word to complete each sentence.

Can you teach me how to read and spell? spell/space
I had a snack before lunch today. snap/snack
Have you ever seen a white squirrel? squirrel/squirm
Mary spilled ice cream on her dress. spice/spilled
When you sneeze, please cover your mouth. snuggle/sneeze

2 Add the letters **squ** to complete each word. Then circle the word that rhymes with "please" and draw a rectangle around the word that names a shape.

squ
squash
squeeze
squat
squirt
squeak
square

3 Draw a line from each picture to the blend at the end of its name.

elf
branch
salt
nch
lt
lf
shelf
bench
belt

4 Find the words from the box in the word search below.

melt lunch myself flow adult

f	l	o	w	f	o
m	y	s	e	l	f
e	b	q	u	n	t
l	u	n	c	h	h
t	a	d	u	l	t

31

Write the blends **sn**, **sp**, and **squ** each on separate index cards. Put the cards into a bag. Let your child select a card and pronounce the blend. Next, tell your child to search around the house to find things whose names begin with each blend. Alternatively, you could use other blends such as **cl**, **br**, **pl**, and **gr**.

32

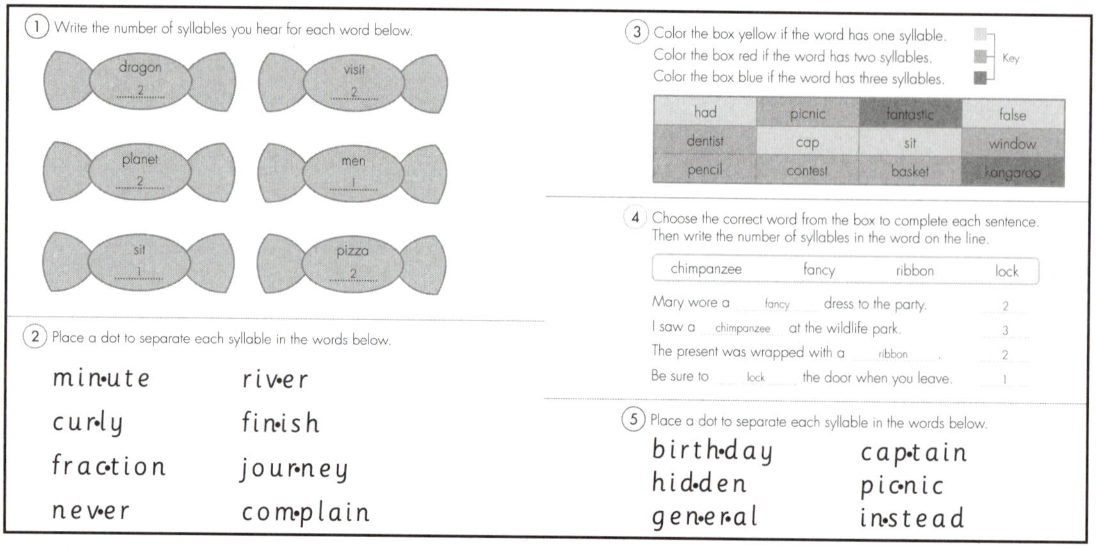

1 Write the number of syllables you hear for each word below.

dragon 2
visit 2
planet 2
men 1
sit 1
pizza 2

2 Place a dot to separate each syllable in the words below.

min•ute riv•er
cur•ly fin•ish
frac•tion jour•ney
nev•er com•plain

3 Color the box yellow if the word has one syllable.
Color the box red if the word has two syllables.
Color the box blue if the word has three syllables.
Key

had	picnic	fantastic	false
dentist	cap	sit	window
pencil	contest	basket	kangaroo

4 Choose the correct word from the box to complete each sentence. Then write the number of syllables in the word on the line.

chimpanzee fancy ribbon lock

Mary wore a fancy dress to the party. 2
I saw a chimpanzee at the wildlife park. 3
The present was wrapped with a ribbon. 2
Be sure to lock the door when you leave. 1

5 Place a dot to separate each syllable in the words below.

birth•day cap•tain
hid•den pic•nic
gen•er•al in•stead

33

Say a list of words to your child. Have him or her write them on a piece of paper, one syllable at a time. Then have your child circle the words in which the first syllable has a short vowel sound.

Answers:

34–35 More Syllables

36–37 Double Consonants

34

35

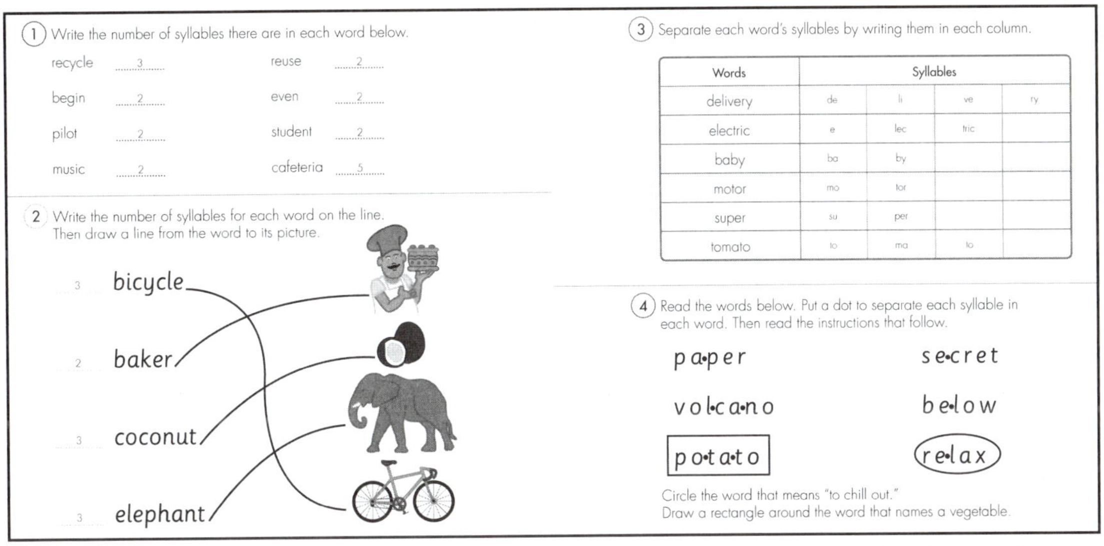

1 Write the number of syllables there are in each word below.

recycle	3	reuse	2
begin	2	even	2
pilot	2	student	2
music	2	cafeteria	5

2 Write the number of syllables for each word on the line. Then draw a line from the word to its picture.

3 bicycle

2 baker

3 coconut

3 elephant

3 Separate each word's syllables by writing them in each column.

Words	Syllables			
delivery	de	li	ve	ry
electric	e	lec	tric	
baby	ba	by		
motor	mo	tor		
super	su	per		
tomato	to	ma	to	

4 Read the words below. Put a dot to separate each syllable in each word. Then read the instructions that follow.

pa•per se•cret

vol•ca•no be•low

po•ta•to re•lax

Circle the word that means "to chill out."

Draw a rectangle around the word that names a vegetable.

Have your child write: "tiger," "dragon," "music," "humor," "visit," "icy," "future," "program," "river," "erase," and "photo." Let your child read each word aloud and decide if the first syllable of each word is an open syllable (ends with a vowel) or closed syllable (ends with a consonant). If needed, use a dictionary for help.

36

37

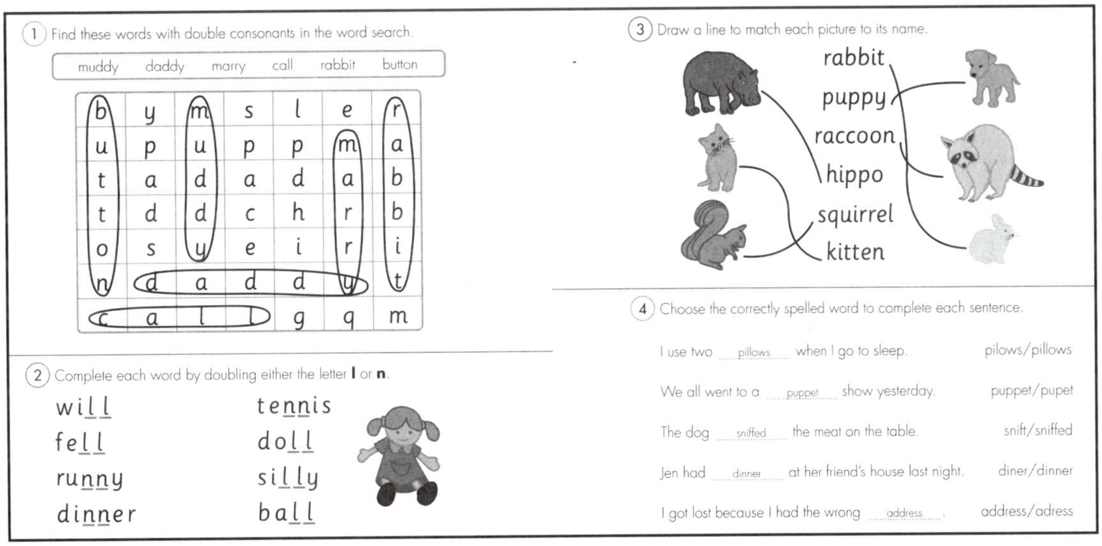

1 Find these words with double consonants in the word search.

muddy daddy marry call rabbit button

b	y	m	s	l	e	r
u	p	u	p	p	m	a
t	a	d	a	d	a	b
t	d	d	c	h	r	b
o	s	y	e	i	r	i
n	d	a	d	d	y	t
c	a	l	l	g	q	m

2 Complete each word by doubling either the letter **l** or **n**.

will tennis

fell doll

runny silly

dinner ball

3 Draw a line to match each picture to its name.

rabbit

puppy

raccoon

hippo

squirrel

kitten

4 Choose the correctly spelled word to complete each sentence.

I use two pillows when I go to sleep. pilows/pillows

We all went to a puppet show yesterday. puppet/pupet

The dog sniffed the meat on the table. snift/sniffed

Jen had dinner at her friend's house last night. diner/dinner

I got lost because I had the wrong address. address/adress

With your child, look around your home for items whose names include a double consonant. These items could include a battery, apple, kettle, mattress, and pillow.

Answers:

38–39 Compound Words

40–41 Plural Endings

38

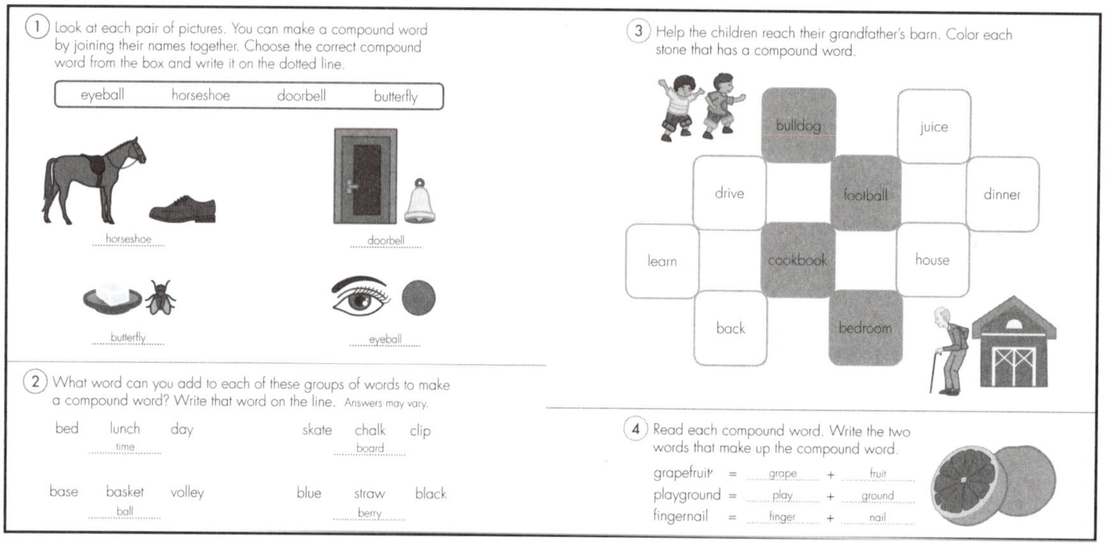
1 Look at each pair of pictures. You can make a compound word by joining their names together. Choose the correct compound word from the box and write it on the dotted line.

eyeball horseshoe doorbell butterfly

horseshoe

doorbell

butterfly

eyeball

2 What word can you add to each of these groups of words to make a compound word? Write that word on the line. Answers may vary.

bed lunch day — time

skate chalk clip — board

base basket volley — ball

blue straw black — berry

3 Help the children reach their grandfather's barn. Color each stone that has a compound word.

bulldog juice drive football dinner learn cookbook house back bedroom

4 Read each compound word. Write the two words that make up the compound word.

grapefruit = grape + fruit

playground = play + ground

fingernail = finger + nail

39

Let your child use old magazines to cut out pictures that illustrate each part of a compound word. Your child can then glue them onto strips of paper and write the compound word below the pictures.

40

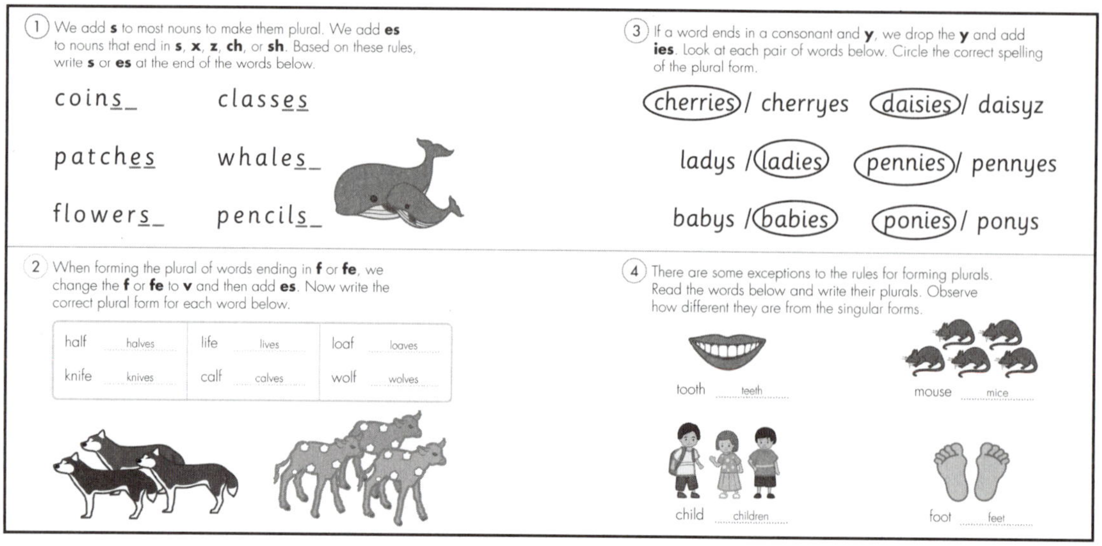
1 We add **s** to most nouns to make them plural. We add **es** to nouns that end in **s**, **x**, **z**, **ch**, or **sh**. Based on these rules, write **s** or **es** at the end of the words below.

coins classes

patches whales

flowers pencils

2 When forming the plural of words ending in **f** or **fe**, we change the **f** or **fe** to **v** and then add **es**. Now write the correct plural form for each word below.

half	halves	life	lives	loaf	loaves
knife	knives	calf	calves	wolf	wolves

3 If a word ends in a consonant and **y**, we drop the **y** and add **ies**. Look at each pair of words below. Circle the correct spelling of the plural form.

cherries / cherryes daisies / daisyz

ladys / ladies pennies / pennyes

babys / babies ponies / ponys

4 There are some exceptions to the rules for forming plurals. Read the words below and write their plurals. Observe how different they are from the singular forms.

tooth teeth

mouse mice

child children

foot feet

41

Write a variety of plural words on small pieces of paper and place them in a bag. Let your child pick one word at a time out of the bag and then tell you its singular form.

Answers:

42–43 Prefix Power

44–45 Useful Word List 2, see p.80

46–47 Suffixes

42

1 The prefix **pre** added to a word can mean "before." The prefix **un** added to a word can mean "not." Add **un** or **pre** to the words below to make new words.

unhappy	unkind	preview
unfair	preschool	unlike

2 The prefix **non** added to a word can mean "without." The prefix **bi** added to a word can mean "two." Sort the words from the box under the two headings **non** and **bi** to make new words.

fiction monthly cycle sense weekly stop

non	bi
nonsense	biweekly
nonfiction	bimonthly
nonstop	bicycle

3 The prefix **sub** added to a word can mean "under." Draw a line from each word to its meaning.

subzero	vehicle for under the sea
submerge	put under water
submarine	under zero

43

4 The prefix **dis** added to a word can mean "the opposite of." Check (✔) the box with the correct meaning for each word below.

dislike
- to not like ✔
- to not dive

disobey
- to not care
- to not obey ✔

dishonest
- without honor
- without honesty ✔

disappear
- to not appear ✔
- to not hear

5 Choose words from the box to complete each sentence.

mistake unavailable returned unable

Today, I returned to the shoe store.

But I was unable to find the green shoes I saw last week.

The clerk told me that they were now unavailable.

It was a mistake not to buy them earlier.

Write words with prefixes on index cards. Cut the cards, separating the prefix from the remainder, or root word. Mix up all the cards and have your child draw cards from a pile and assemble them into words. Invite your child to use each word in a sentence.

46

1 The suffix **able** added to a word can mean "able to." The suffix **less** added to a word can mean "without." Draw a line to match each word to its meaning.

hopeless	able to be washed
enjoyable	without spots
washable	without hope
spotless	able to be enjoyed

2 The suffix **ness** added to a word can mean "a state of being." The suffix **ment** added to a word can mean "an act or happening." The suffix **ful** added to a word can mean "full of." Write the words from the box under the suffixes **ment**, **ness**, or **ful**.

amuse fear kind happy treat sad joy pay cheer

ment	ness	ful
amusement	happiness	fearful
payment	sadness	joyful
treatment	kindness	cheerful

47

3 The suffix **est** added to a word can mean "most." Complete each set by writing the third word.

close	closer	closest	happy	happier	happiest
soft	softer	softest	light	lighter	lightest

4 Match each description to the word it describes. Write the number of the word next to the correct letter. To check your answers, add the numbers in each column and row. They should be the same!

A. full of grace	1. happiness
B. state of being dark	2. enjoyment
C. act of enjoying	3. treatment
D. act of treating	4. graceful
E. full of care	5. careful
F. able to be washed	6. luckiest
G. able to agree	7. washable
H. state of being happy	8. agreeable
I. most lucky	9. darkness

A. 4	B. 9	C. 2
D. 3	E. 5	F. 7
G. 8	H. 1	I. 6

Write words with suffixes on index cards. Write the meaning of each word on other index cards. Arrange the cards facedown. Let your child turn two cards over at a time to play a memory game. Give your child two points for each card and definition he or she matches correctly.

Answers:

48–49 Homophones

50–51 Antonyms

48

(1) Choose the correct word to complete each sentence.

The players choose the best bats and balls. chews/choose

They're always determined to win. There/They're

You'll never see them give up. sea/see

They always keep their eye on the ball. eye/I

(2) In each row, find the pairs of words and phrases that go together. Color the boxes with those pairs in each row the same color.

sent	an odor	mailed	scent
piece of wood	not interested	bored	board
hair	hare	covers the scalp	animal like a rabbit
not strong	week	weak	seven days
part of a plant	flower	finely ground grain	flour
heel	back part of foot	to get better	heal

49

(3) Circle the homophones in each sentence.

We are (allowed) to speak (aloud.)

We (know) that (no) other team is like ours.

John (threw) the ball a long way (through) the air.

He (rose) from his seat to give the speaker a (rose.)

(4) Write a homophone for each word below.

blew blue

peace piece

write right

male mail

sum some

Make some sentences using two homophones, as in question 3 above. Say them aloud to your child and let him or her identify the homophones and then spell them out to you.

50

(1) Draw a line from each word to its antonym.

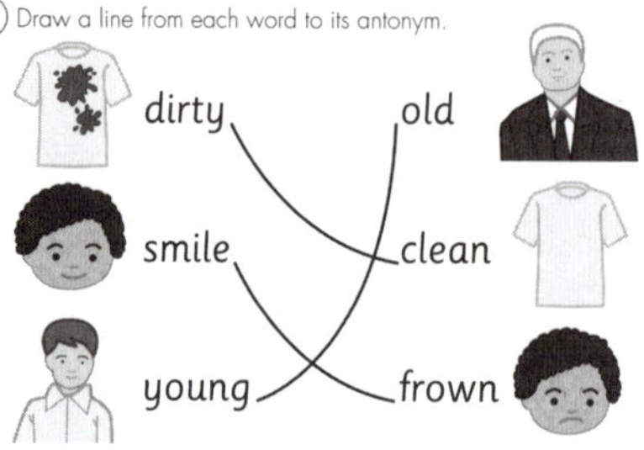

(2) Look at the pictures of the food items and read their descriptions. Write an antonym for the underlined word.

sour juice sweet

straight fries curly

thin smoothie thick

worst hot dog best

51

(3) Circle the antonym for the underlined word in each sentence below.

Someone had left the door open, but Jon wanted it (shut).

We got to the fair (early) and stayed until late that night.

We crossed the bridge over the river and took the tunnel (under) the road.

(4) Write the antonym for the underlined word in each sentence below.

Dad has already mowed the upper lawn and is now mowing the lower part.

Jan is not in front of me but is somewhere behind me.

If you cannot fix my bike, it will break my heart.

My brother likes to eat cold pizza, but I prefer hot pizza.

My dog is sad when he is alone, but he is happy when I play with him.

Let your child draw pictures to show things whose names are opposites. For example, he or she might draw a boy walking up some steps and a girl coming down them or a white house with a black dog. Encourage your child to be creative in his or her drawings.

Answers:

52–53 Synonyms

54–55 Verb Endings

52

1 For each sentence, write a word from the box that is the synonym for the underlined word.

relax | prepare | glance | heats

Mother will make dinner soon. prepare
The sun warms the ground. heats
Take a look at that large dog. glance
Let's rest before we go out again. relax

2 Choose two words that are synonyms from the word box. Then write them in pairs below.

injured | choose | tired | weary | hurt | select

injured / hurt — weary / tired — choose / select

3 Circle the synonym for the underlined word in each sentence below.

Tom saw a small purple stone in the (little) pond.

The present was beautifully wrapped at the (gift) shop.

53

4 Help Patrick the pink rabbit hop his way through the maze to reach the tasty carrots. Color only the boxes that have true statements.

A synonym for "answer" is "reply."
Another word for "city" is "country."
Another word for "idea" is "thought."
A synonym for "still" is "silent."
The opposite of "sea" is "ocean."
An antonym for "above" is "below."
Another word for "near" is "far."
A synonym for "happy" is "glad."
An antonym for "tiny" is "small."
An antonym for "find" is "lose."
An antonym for "job" is "work."
Another word for "happy" is "sad."
Another word for "border" is "edge."
The opposite of "find" is "locate."
The antonym for "child" is "adult."

Draw a square 10 inches by 10 inches and divide it into nine boxes. In each box, write a word that has a synonym. On index cards, write a synonym for each of the nine words in the boxes. Turn the cards facedown. Let him or her read the words in the boxes first and then turn over a card. Your child should match the card to its synonym in one of the boxes. Continue until all the word cards and boxes are paired up.

54

1 Look at each word below. Drop the verb ending for each and write the root word (infinitive) on the line.

explored explore
walked walk
painting paint
studied study

2 Find the verb in each sentence. Circle its **ing** or **ed** ending.

Jan slipp(ed) on the icy sidewalk.

Joe plann(ed) a trip to California.

Are you go(ing) to the beach now?

Jake finally finish(ed) his homework at 7 o'clock.

I am draw(ing) a picture for my art class.

55

3 Color the six boxes that have correctly spelled verbs.

learning	takeing	stopping	tradeing
carrying	singging	humming	runing
counting	flying	choping	spending

Write the correct spelling for the other six words below.

taking | trading | singing
running | counting | chopping

4 Add **ed** to each root word below. **Remember:** you may have to double some consonants first!

watch ed | start ed | drop ped
want ed | slap ped | crash ed

5 Add **ied** to each root word below. **Remember:** drop the **y** first!

carry carried | worry worried
cry cried | try tried
hurry hurried | marry married

Prepare two sets of cards. One set should show the endings **ed**, **ing**, **ied**, and **s**. The other set should show root verbs, such as "carry," "shout," and "run." Place the cards in two piles. Let your child sort the cards to make words and write them on paper.

Answers:

56–57 The Letters **c** and **g**

58–59 Which Word?

56

1. Find the word in each row that is spelled correctly. Circle the word and say it aloud.

ciicle	cyycle	(cycle)
(page)	paage	pag
coyn	(coin)	coiin

2. Choose the correct word to complete each sentence below.

I picked the salad with celery. — selery/celery
She likes a lot of ice in her drink. — ice/ize
Please give me a large helping. — large/lurge
They will form the government. — govenment/government

3. Circle the incorrectly spelled word in each row below.

caught	(centur)	coach
(jentle)	giant	game
going	(giive)	gang

57

4. Color the box if the word in it is spelled correctly. Put an **X** on the incorrectly spelled word. Then write the correct words below.

frog	cake	carry	~~genral~~
~~silk~~	~~jinjer~~	~~kave~~	dance

silk ginger cave general

5. Draw a line from the picture to its name only if it is spelled correctly.

Make a list of hard and soft **c** and **g** words for your child. Ask him or her to circle the words with the soft sound and underline the words with the hard sound.

58

1. Read each sentence. Find the one word that is spelled incorrectly in the sentence. Underline it and then write it correctly on the line.

I am a <u>hapy</u> person. — happy
They are <u>runing</u> quickly — running
Tom told a <u>funy</u> joke. — funny
Mary is <u>rideing</u> a bike. — riding

2. Choose the correctly spelled verb, or action word, to complete each sentence.

We ran to the store to buy ice cream. — by/buy
His father drove home after the game. — droove/drove
Jim baked cookies for the school sale. — baked/bakt
Joan liked to fish and wade in the stream. — waade/wade

3. Write your own adjective, or describing word, to complete each sentence. Use a dictionary to check the spelling. Answers may vary.

Mom baked a .... birthday cake for me.
The cheese sandwiches were very ....
Sally took a .... trip to the zoo.
The eagle had .... wings.

59

4. Read the ten naming words, or nouns, in the box and then find them in the word search.

pavement key library
crab drum towel fuzz
carrot wheat river

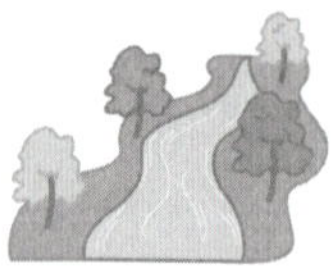

p	x	c	c	a	r	r	o	t
a	o	p	b	a	i	f	l	k
v	d	r	u	m	v	u	i	g
e	d	a	h	r	e	z	b	e
m	k	e	y	t	r	z	r	t
e	k	d	s	x	c	o	a	o
n	i	u	x	w	r	d	r	w
t	q	z	p	r	a	k	y	e
w	h	e	a	t	b	n	m	l

Write three or four describing words (adjectives) on a piece of paper. Then ask your child to think of a word that names a person, a place, and a thing to go with each describing word. For example: a huge person, a giant place, a green apple, and so on.

Answers:

60–61 Sentence Sense

62–63 Spelling Sense

64–65 Useful Word List 3, see p.80

60

1) Read each sentence below. Circle the incorrectly spelled word. Then write it correctly on the line.

We are having our (schull) picnic tomorrow. school

Where is the picnic going to be (helled)? held

What are you (takeing) to the picnic? taking

I am (worryed) about what I should take. worried

Maybe I will take a (lemin) cake. lemon

Let's hope it doesn't (rayne) tomorrow. rain

61

2) When you write sentences, you use **who**, **when**, and **where** words. Correct the spelling for each word in the box and then write it under one of the three headings.

wryter	artest	toodae	tommorrow	nerse
danser	aftre	citie	teecher	beforr
purson	libarry	sisstur	Febuary	offiss
iland	dezert	parc	Sonday	peeple
Fryday	yustrday	outdores	hoam	unkle
skool	Oggust	faather	muzeam	evrydae

Who	When	Where
person	after	city
sister	yesterday	library
dancer	today	outdoors
nurse	tomorrow	office
teacher	before	island
writer	Sunday	desert
artist	Friday	museum
people	February	home
uncle	everyday	school
father	August	park

Help your child improve his or her spelling and vocabulary. Say a word such as "wealthy." Ask your child to make up a sentence using a synonym for "wealthy," such as "rich." Continue with other words. You can also use words that have antonyms in this exercise, such as "front" and "back."

62

Read the story below and then answer the questions that follow.

Wonderful Trees

Trees are wonderful. They help our Earth and all living things. Do you no how they help?

Trees help kleen our air. They take in a harmful gas from the air and use it to make their own food. The trees use the fod. The leaves give off a clean gas for people to breathe.

Trees do many other helpful things. Their leaves give us shade from the sun. Trees give workers wood to build houses and other things. Some parts of a tree are used to make the paper we write on.

Trees also give animals homes. Woodpeckers use holes in trees to make nests for their babies. Squirrels build nests high in the branches of trees. They store nuts in tree holes and eat them during the cold winter when food is hard to find. Owls use twigs from trees to make their nests. Insects such as beetles live on or under the bark of trees. A mother fox will sometimes use a hollow tree trunk as a den for her cubs.

Trees do so many things for our world. What would we do without them?

63

1) Find the word in line 2 that is spelled incorrectly. Correct it here.

know

2) Find the incorrectly spelled word in line 3. Write the correct spelling here.

clean

3) Look at line 4. Find the word to which you need to add another **o** to correct its spelling. Write it correctly here.

food

4) Which of these is the correct spelling of the word? Circle it.

shayd (shade) shede

5) The word "nests" is in the story. Write a rhyming word for it.
Answers may vary.

pests

6) "Sometimes" is made up of two words. Think of another word that is made up of two words. Write it here. Answers will vary.

butterfly

After your child has completed the exercises, you could ask him or her questions to check his or her understanding of the text. You could also ask your child to tell you a synonym or an antonym of some of the words used, such as "clean," "helpful," "high," and "many," and then to spell it out.

Answers:

20–21 Useful word list 1

44–45 Useful word list 2

64–65 Useful word list 3

20

able	able	growl	growl	chirp	chirp	radio	radio
cucumber	cucumber	climb	climb	hiss	hiss	decide	decide
known	known	against	against	idea	idea	artist	artist
smooth	smooth	rustle	rustle	toast	toast	special	special
thumb	thumb	edge	edge	editor	editor	though	though
bare	bare	follow	follow	bought	bought	balloon	balloon
elevate	elevate	agree	agree	neither	neither	island	island
bloom	bloom	pour	pour	o'clock	o'clock	unknown	unknown
library	library	field	field	poem	poem	young	young
chief	chief	believe	believe	enough	enough	writer	writer

21

The method of learning to spell using look, say, cover, write, and check is a familiar practice for many children. Encourage your child to frequently return to the Useful Word Lists on pages 20–21, 44–45, and 64–65. Test your child until he or she can spell and write all those words with confidence and accuracy. Each time, praise progress and improvement.

44

describe	describe	champion	champion	bulb	bulb	calm	calm
ache	ache	guitar	guitar	faint	faint	jungle	jungle
knife	knife	liquid	liquid	ceiling	ceiling	aim	aim
comb	comb	collar	collar	bait	bait	desert	desert
autumn	autumn	biscuit	biscuit	fright	fright	knight	knight
fierce	fierce	aloud	aloud	lamb	lamb	label	label
banquet	banquet	majesty	majesty	foam	foam	envelope	envelope
equal	equal	design	design	ghost	ghost	level	level
journey	journey	invisible	invisible	drift	drift	eagle	eagle
burrow	burrow	gasp	gasp	handle	handle	museum	museum

45

64

could	could	Monday	Monday	January	January	November	November
should	should	Tuesday	Tuesday	February	February	December	December
would	would	Wednesday	Wednesday	March	March	month	month
very	very	Thursday	Thursday	April	April	year	year
every	every	Friday	Friday	May	May	school	school
other	other	Saturday	Saturday	June	June	rain	rain
another	another	Sunday	Sunday	July	July	cloud	cloud
because	because	today	today	August	August	snow	snow
open	open	tomorrow	tomorrow	September	September	wind	wind
close	close	yesterday	yesterday	October	October	weather	weather

65